LATINOS IN BASEBALL

Vinny Castilla

Tony DeMarco

Mitchell Lane Publishers, Inc.
P.O. Box 200
Childs, MD 21916-0200

LATINOS IN BASEBALL

Tino Martinez	Bobby Bonilla	Roberto Alomar	Pedro Martinez
Moises Alou	Sammy Sosa	Ivan Rodriguez	Bernie Williams
Ramon Martinez	Alex Rodriguez	**Vinny Castilla**	Manny Ramirez

First Printing

Library of Congress Cataloging-in-Publication Data

DeMarco, Tony (Anthony P.)
    Vinny Castilla / Tony DeMarco.
        p. cm. — (Latinos in baseball)
    Includes index.
    Summary: A biography of the dedicated player from Mexico who is now the aggressive-hitting third baseman for the Colorado Rockies.
    ISBN 1-58415-008-4
    1. Castilla, Vinny, 1967—Juvenile literature. 2. Baseball players—Mexico—Biography—Juvenile literature. [1. Castilla, Vinny, 1967- 2. Baseball players. 3. Mexican Americans—Biography.] I. Title. II. Series.
GV865.C35 D46 2000
796.357'092—dc21
    [B]
                                      99-053142

About the Author: Tony DeMarco is a freelance writer who has covered major-league baseball since 1985 for the *Denver Post, MSNBC Online*, the *Fort Worth Star Telegram*, and the *Miami Herald*. He has also authored biographies of Ivan Rodriguez, Larry Walker, and Ed McCaffrey. His articles have appeared in *The Sporting News, Sport Magazine, Beckett's Baseball, The Complete Handbook of Baseball*, and *Peterson's Baseball*. He lives in Englewood, Colorado.

Photo Credits: cover: Tim DeFrisco/Allsport; p. 4 Brian Bahr/Allsport; pp. 6, 8, 10 ©1998 Rich Clarkson and Associates; p. 25 Steve Dunn/Allsport; p. 27 Dan Levine/Archive Photos; pp. 29, 35, 39, 43 ©1998 Rich Clarkson and Associates; p. 45 Shaun Best/Archive Photos; p. 48 Brian Bahr/Allsport; pp. 50, 55, 57 ©1998 Rich Clarkson and Associates; p. 59 Brian Bahr/Allsport.

Acknowledgments: The following story was developed based on personal interviews with Vinny Castilla on April 18, May 23, June 24, and August 9, 1999. Professional and personal friends were also interviewed for this book, including Bob Gebhard (April 15, 1999), Don Baylor (April 18, 1999) and Bobby Cox (April 18, 1999). This story has been thoroughly researched and checked for accuracy. To the best of our knowledge, it represents a true story. The author and publisher wish to thank Vinny Castilla for his cooperation and helpfulness in the development of this book.

TABLE OF CONTENTS

Vinny Castilla has come a long way from a small town in southern Mexico and now is regarded as one of the best third basemen in the major leagues.

CHAPTER ONE
National Hero

T he streets of Monterrey, Mexico, jumped with excitement and anticipation. Easter Sunday, April 4, 1999, was an historic day in Vinny Castilla's native country, but it had nothing to do with religion. Hero-worship maybe.

This was about baseball, and more specifically, the return of a native son. Major-league teams had traveled south of the border for exhibition games a handful of times previously. The San Diego Padres and New York Mets had played a three-game regular-season series in Monterrey in 1998. But this was even bigger.

The Major League Baseball season was going to begin off American soil for the first time in history, and the game would feature Mexico's biggest star—Vinny Castilla—who had returned with his Colorado Rockies teammates to play the Padres, a World Series participant the previous October.

Estadio Monterrey, normally the home of the Monterrey Sultanes of the Mexican League, had been sold out just three hours after tickets went on sale, even though ticket prices in the 27,000-seat stadium ranged up to the equivalent of $60 in American money.

It didn't matter that Vinny had been born in Oaxaca (pronounced Wa-*ha*-ka), a city in the state of Oaxaca, which is located in the southern part of Mexico, and that Monterrey was 900 miles to the north in the state of Nuevo Leon, about 150 miles south of the Mexico-Texas border.

With more home runs than any player ever to come from Mexico, Vinny is a national hero in his native country.

Vinny, the best major-league hitter ever to come out of Mexico, was being treated like a local hero. The front page of the local sports section featured a picture of Vinny wearing a black suit and black wing-tip shoes, swinging a bat in the batter's box. The headline in all capital letters read: CLASE Y PODER. Translated: "Class and Power."

Fans arrived very early to catch a glimpse of their hero, and with music blaring, the atmosphere in Estadio Monterrey was festive. Typical of his humble nature, Vinny chose that night to wear uniform No. 14 instead of his usual No. 9, in honor of close friend and former teammate Andres Galarraga, who had just been stricken with cancer and was unable to play the 1999 season.

Among those watching that night were Vinny's family: father Carlos, mother Carmelita, brother Carlos Jr., sister Eleyna, and wife Samantha, plus many other relatives and friends from Oaxaca—not to mention national television audiences in Mexico and the United States. Even Vinny's father was overwhelmed by well-wishers and autograph seekers.

"I'm very proud of him," Carlos told an American newspaper reporter. "I could never dream that Vinny would be like a hero in our country. Everybody wants to know about Vinny. I'm his father, and they want my autograph."

Vinny told a television interviewer before the game, "It is amazing to me. I never thought I would be playing a game like this in my home country. It's crazy to me." And then he went out and played a game that his fellow countrymen could be proud of, leading the Rockies to an 8-2 victory.

On the very first pitch Vinny saw from Padres right-hander Andy Ashby in the top of the first inning, he hit a ground ball in the hole between third base and shortstop for an infield single. Vinny popped out to shortstop in his second at-bat, which came in the Rockies' five-run second inning, but he was far from finished.

He hit a line-drive single to left field in the fourth inning; got another infield single in the sixth

Though not a particularly large man by today's standards, Vinny has great power due to his bat speed and strong forearms and wrists.

inning on a bad-hop ground ball that eluded Padres third baseman George Arias; and in his final at-bat lined a double into the left-field corner to go 4 for 5 with one run scored. The only thing missing was a home run.

"I really wanted to hit a home run, but it was great fun," Vinny said. "I tried on my last two at-bats. I would have loved to have played the whole series here. I'll remember a lot—the win, the cheers they gave me. It was something I'll always remember.

"The whole country is behind me. Everybody loves me there. I'm happy for their support. It gives me motivation to play hard for those people. They buy satellite dishes so they can watch my games. It's an extra push to have that kind of support from your country."

Even though San Diego sits just north of the Mexico–United States border, the crowd cheered loudly for the Rockies—especially Vinny. What impressed Rockies players and team officials most about their two-day stay south of the border was how adored Vinny is in his home country.

"Some of the fans were for us, and some of the fans were for San Diego, but everybody was for Vinny," Rockies manager Jim Leyland told reporters afterward. "It was Vinny's night. I'll remember that I was part of history. I hope my kids will be able to look in the baseball encyclopedia someday and see what happened here."

Outfielder Curtis Goodwin had seen it all before. He previously had played with Vinny on a Mexican Winter League team in Obregon.

Adored in his native Mexico and very popular in Colorado, Vinny always takes time to sign autographs for his fans.

"I've hung around with Michael Jordan, and I haven't seen anything like it," Goodwin said. "It was crazy. We'd try to leave the stadium, and the people would be across the street, and bring the whole street with them. Vinny would roll down his window and sign for everybody. I guess when you're representing your whole country, it's a different story."

Added general manager Bob Gebhard: "My first impression in trying to describe it is that Vinny is somewhere between Abraham Lincoln, John F. Kennedy and Babe Ruth. I thought he handled everything great. There were a lot of things he was asked to do. There was a lot of pressure on him. And he was so gracious. He thinks so much of his fellow countrymen, he agreed to do everything he was asked to do.

"Even now, he still goes back every year and plays winter ball for a couple of weeks because he feels he owes it to his people. We could stop it, but we know that it's good for Vinny, and it's good for the country of Mexico. That tells you something about him. Vinny is special. He is a special individual."

—A special individual from very humble beginnings.

CHAPTER TWO
Humble Beginnings

C arlos Castilla was a teacher at an elementary school in Oaxaca, making enough money to keep his three children well fed and clothed. In Oaxaca, a poor state filled with native Mexicans who produced pottery, crafts and leather goods, that was more than many.

When Carlos made time for his two boys— Carlos Jr., and Vinicio Soria Castilla, (born July 4, 1967), in Oaxaca—they would often go to a nearby playground and practice baseball. Although Carlos Sr. had been a good player on the local level, he did not advance any further. But right away, Vinicio showed great talent and affection for the game.

"My dad played baseball. When you're a kid, you do what your dad did," Vinny said. "I started playing baseball, and I liked it. I played soccer in school, too, because we didn't have baseball in the schools. More kids like soccer in Oaxaca. They like more action. To have fun in baseball, you have to know how to play."

Even playing against older boys, Vinny was a standout. He played Little League baseball every Saturday, always at shortstop. But if a boy in Oaxaca dreamed about playing professional baseball, it was as a player in the Mexican League, and not the big leagues in the United States.

"Even the Mexican League seemed so far away," Vinny said. "I was just a guy from Oaxaca. It's a small town. It's not even a baseball town. It's more of a soccer town. It's far down south in Mexico, and that's more of a soccer area. Baseball is more popular in the northern part of the country. Now, they have a pro baseball team in Oaxaca, but back then we didn't.

"I had heard of Hector Espino [the Mexican League's all-time home run leader]. But I was a shortstop, so I liked other shortstops. One of them was Houston Jimenez, who played a couple of years with the Minnesota Twins. As I got older, I started following Fernando Valenzuela and Teddy Higuera. But the big leagues seemed so far away at that time."

Vinny graduated from Carlos Gracida Institute (the equivalent of high school) in 1985 and was the baseball team's most valuable player that year. He went on to Benito Juárez University, a school named for Oaxaca's most famous citizen and former president of Mexico, all the while playing for a semi-pro team close to home.

Those games were watched closely by scouts from Mexican League teams, and Vinny was impressive enough to be a first-round draft choice of the Saltillo Sarapemakers. It was during his three years with Saltillo that Vinny struck up a friendship with a pitcher on his team, Armando Reynoso, who currently pitches for the Arizona Diamondbacks. Their career paths would keep them playing together for most of the next decade, and the two have remained best friends.

The Mexican League is divided by seasons. There is a summer league and a winter league. The summer league offers younger players a chance to prove themselves, while the winter league is a bit tougher because it includes Mexican-born major-leaguers who are home for the winter, as well as minor-league players from the United States who are trying to improve their game. The winter league also has fewer teams, and therefore fewer roster spots to fill. As a young player, Vinny played in the summer league for three seasons. During this time he began considering a baseball career and the possibility of playing in the major leagues.

"I started thinking, 'I want to go to the States,'" he said. "'I know I can play in the Mexican League. I want to go to another level. I want to see how far I can go.' I wanted to try. I wanted the opportunity."

But that opportunity wasn't quick in coming. As a 6-foot-1-inch, 160-pound shortstop, Vinny attended one tryout camp that was run by a hand-ful of major-league teams. He did well, but he wasn't signed. Meanwhile, he saw other players he thought he was better than get the chance to go to the United States to play.

"I started getting frustrated," Vinny said. "I showed everything that I had, and they would sign somebody else before me. I would think, 'That player didn't have better talent than me, but they signed him and not me. What's going on?'"

In Mexico, players' rights are held by the team they play for, and any American team that wants to sign a player has to pay the Mexican team that owns him. Vinny grew so frustrated, he thought that per-haps the owner of the Saltillo team wanted too much money from an American team to let him go. But the owner said that was not the case.

Vinny's opportunity finally came after the 1989 summer season. He hit .307 with 25 doubles, 13 triples, 10 homers and 58 RBIs in 128 games, and he made the All-Star Game that season. At-lanta Braves scout Jack Pierce, a former outfielder who had spent three years in the majors with At-lanta and Detroit, recommended the club try to sign Vinny, and after farm director Paul Snyder went to Mexico to see Vinny for himself, they offered the owner of the Saltillo club $20,000 for Vinny's contract. Of that amount, only 25 percent went to Vinny, who after taxes was left with only about $3,000. But he would have gone for nothing, because it was the opportunity he had been seeking.

Vinny's first step would be to play in the two-month-long fall instructional league at the Braves' West Palm Beach training headquarters. But there was a snag—he didn't have the working visa required for nonresidents coming into the United States. Pierce had purchased a plane ticket for Vinny to fly from Monterrey to West Palm Beach, but without a visa, Vinny wouldn't be allowed into the country.

What Vinny did have was a border-crossing permit, which he had obtained because his Saltillo team regularly crossed the border into the United States to play in Laredo, Texas. So Pierce and Vinny crossed the border at Laredo, then made the three-hour drive to San Antonio, where Vinny caught a flight to West Palm Beach.

"That's how I got into the States," Vinny said.

Little did he know that he was about to embark on a long and sometimes frustrating journey that would eventually lead him to hero status in his native land.

CHAPTER THREE
A Long Way From Home

For a 22-year-old who spoke few words of English, the transition from Oaxaca to West Palm Beach was difficult. Vinny's days were all the same, revolving around baseball and the Days Inn, where he and other players were housed. He would have breakfast at a buffet provided by the Braves in the hotel, go to the ballpark for the day, then return to the hotel for dinner.

Once in a while, when he was still hungry, Vinny would go across the street to a fast-food restaurant with some of the other Latin players who spoke English, and they would order for him. The monotonous schedule began to wear on him.

"The two months in the instructional league were pretty long for me," Vinny said. "It seemed like two years. It was a different country, a different culture. The American players, the ones who were drafted by the Braves, were driving brand-new cars, and they would go out at night.

"But I didn't do anything. I didn't go out. I hardly ever left the hotel. Me and another player, Gerardo Cantu, would stay in and watch movies. Maybe we would go to the mall once in a while. But we didn't have any money. They only gave us five dollars a day. That was tough. But I told myself that if I wanted to be in the big leagues, I had to sacrifice."

Vinny played well enough to be assigned to the Braves' lower Class-A farm team in Sumter, South Carolina, the following spring. Off the field, the situation was much the same as it had been in West Palm Beach. Vinny still spoke little English and made very little money, and Sumter was a very small town with little to do.

Even though he was doing well on the field, Vinny looked at the difficult road ahead and wondered whether the strange surroundings and tough circumstances were worth the effort. He was making only $800 a month, while back home in Mexico, where he was already a star player, he had been making the equivalent of $2,000 per month.

"Most of the time, teams take a player up one classification per year," Vinny said. "I was thinking, this is low-A ball. Next year would be high A, then 1992 would be Double-A, 1993 would be Triple-A, then maybe the big leagues. I was looking at five years, and that was if everything goes good. I thought to myself, I'm already an all-star in Mexico. Maybe I should go back home."

An embarrassing incident at a local fast-food restaurant intensified Vinny's feelings about returning to Mexico. Up to that point, Latino teammates, particularly catcher Eddie Perez, had ordered Vinny's food for him because Vinny was still unsure of his English. This time, Perez wanted Vinny to try to order for himself. Vinny attempted to order a hamburger and french fries, but the woman behind the counter couldn't understand him and got testy with him.

"Eddie was laughing. My teammates thought it was funny. But I was embarrassed," Vinny said. "There was a big line behind me, too. Now, when Americans go to Mexico to play winter ball, I help them a lot because I know how hard it is."

It was a letter from his father that convinced Vinny to stick it out and, in effect, changed Vinny's life. "My dad said, 'The Braves signed you because they thought you could be a major-league player. Don't leave. The only way you can be a major-league player is if you stay there, so you should stay.' I said, 'He's right. That's true.' I stayed and had a good year. I had to learn the language as well as possible. It wasn't easy for me, but I worked hard at it."

Nine years later, as he watched his son being treated like a national hero in Monterrey, Vinny's father told a reporter, "I told him not to come home. I knew he had potential. I said, 'Give it five years.'"

As it turned out, Vinny was in the majors to stay only three years later. That summer at Sumter, he made the South Atlantic League All-Star team. He hit .268 with nine home runs and 53 RBIs in 93 games before being promoted to Double-A Greenville of the Southern League.

Vinny played 46 games there and hit .235 with four homers and 16 RBIs. He began the 1991 season there as well.

Vinny's stay in Greenville lasted only 66 games into the 1991 season before he was promoted to Triple-A Richmond: he had hit .270 with seven homers and 44 RBIs. In 67 games with Richmond, he hit seven more home runs and drove in 36 more runs, giving him a total of 14 homers and 80 RBIs at the two stops—very good production for a short-stop. The Braves thought enough of Vinny's season to call him up to the majors on September 1. In 12 games, Vinny went 1 for 5, getting his first major-league hit—a single—off Houston's Xavier Hernandez.

Vinny was ready to go back to Mexico and prepare for the winter ball season when the Braves offered a pleasant surprise. They asked him to stick around and work out with the team as it went into postseason play, even though he wouldn't be on the 25-man active roster. Vinny gladly accepted, and watched from the bench as the Braves defeated the Pittsburgh Pirates in the National League Championship Series, four games to three.

That put the Braves, who had finished in last place in 1990, in their first World Series since 1958, when the franchise was located in Milwaukee. Their opponent was the Minnesota Twins, and again, the Series went a dramatic seven games. Four of the last five games were decided on the final pitch, and five of the seven games were decided by one run, with three going into extra innings. But the Twins, behind clutch pitching by Jack Morris and hitting by Kirby Puckett, won Game 7 in their home park to capture the world championship.

"It was very exciting to watch the playoffs and the World Series," Vinny said. "I was ready to go back home. I'm glad they asked me to stay."

And to imagine, only two years earlier, Vinny was playing for Saltillo in the Mexican Summer League, wondering if his chance in the United States would ever come.

Vinny's 1992 season was quite similar to 1991. He spent most of the season back at Triple-A Richmond, hitting .252 with seven homers and 44 RBIs in 127 games, and finished the year by playing nine games for the Braves, who again advanced to the World Series, and this time lost to the Toronto Blue Jays in six games.

At Richmond, Vinny was hitting only .205 as late as June 5, but he got hotter and hotter as each month passed. He hit .320 in August, including a 24-for-59 streak in his final 16 games before being promoted to Atlanta. Between June 18 and his promotion, Vinny did not go two consecutive games without a hit. In nine games for the Braves, Vinny got four hits in 16 at-bats and drove in his first major-league run.

"We lost the World Series again, but I was excited to be there again," Vinny said. "I felt privileged, even though I knew I wouldn't get into any of the games. I felt like I could play in the big leagues, but I knew it would be hard to get that chance with the Braves."

That chance was about to come from somewhere else.

CHAPTER FOUR
A New Place to Call Home

L ess than one month after the 1992 World Series, Major League Baseball held an expansion draft to stock two new National League teams—the Florida Marlins and the Colorado Rockies. For 7 1/2 hours in the grand ballroom of the Marriott Marquis hotel in New York, executives from both teams picked players off the rosters of the 26 established teams, selecting 72 players in all.

Knowing that the Braves and Blue Jays—the World Series participants—were full of talent, the Rockies and Marlins correctly figured there would be quality players those teams could not include among the 15 each team was allowed to protect. Sure enough, with the first pick in the draft, the Rockies selected pitcher David Nied from the Atlanta organization. The Marlins later said they would have picked Nied if the Rockies hadn't. And when their seventh turn came in the second round, the Rockies selected Vinny.

Little did anybody in that room know that with the 40th overall pick in the draft, the Rockies would get a future All-Star and consistent 40-home-run producer, and a third baseman who would put up one of the greatest offensive seasons by anybody who has played that position. The pick would be the best of the 72 in the draft, and the loss of Vinny by the Braves would prove to be the biggest mistake made by any of the established teams.

"We knew Atlanta was loaded," Gebhard said. "So was Toronto. We knew they wouldn't be able to protect all their premium players. With Vinny, we already had drafted Freddie Benavides to be our regular shortstop. He was more proven. But Vinny was a player we liked for the future.

"I saw Vinny in spring training, then during the season, our scouts kept turning in good reports about him. He was a young guy who we thought could be a good offensive player. We liked his tools. We knew he was going to be a good player, but did I ever in my wildest dreams think he would hit 40 home runs three years in a row? I'd like to say I did, but I didn't. If you call and ask the Braves if there was one mistake they made in the expansion draft, I bet they would say it was Vinny."

The Braves did indeed want to keep Vinny, but they also had another future star in their farm system who played the same position—Chipper Jones, who had been the first overall pick in the 1990 amateur draft. They chose to protect Jones, who, like Vinny, is now a perennial All-Star third baseman.

Said Braves manager Bobby Cox: "Bobby Dews was our farm director at the time, and he loved Vinny. We all liked him. He was a shortstop who could hit, and there aren't many of those around. And we thought he could play shortstop at the major-league level, too.

"He didn't have a lot of range for a shortstop, but he was a guy who was smart. He would learn the hitters. He had good hands, and was a great kid. But we could only protect 15, and we just couldn't protect him. We didn't want to give him up."

The Atlanta Braves wanted to keep Vinny, but the Colorado Rockies chose him in the expansion draft. Vinny welcomed the opportunity to play in the majors.

Vinny was playing winter ball in Obregon when he heard the news, and he welcomed the new opportunity to establish himself as a major-league player. Making the transition easier was the fact that the Rockies had also selected his best friend, Armando Reynoso, from the Braves' organization, keeping the two together with a new team.

Vinny made the Rockies out of spring training, but he began the season as the backup to Benavides, a slick fielder who had two years of major-league experience with the Cincinnati Reds prior to being picked by the Rockies.

In the few opportunities he did receive, Vinny showed impressive power for a player who stood only 6-foot-1 and weighed 185 pounds at that point. On April 25, he hit two 425-foot triples off the center-field wall at Mile High Stadium. Two nights later, he hit his first major-league home run off Chicago left-hander Dan Plesac.

"We drafted Vinny to play behind Benavides, but when Vinny played a couple of times, he hit some balls real hard," Rockies manager Don Baylor said. "I said to myself, 'Where is all this power coming from?' I remember seeing Bobby Cox at the winter meetings after the 1993 season, and he told me, 'Man, I tell you, you got a guy I wanted to keep. He's going to hit.'"

Vinny's big opportunity came in early May, when Benavides injured his knee and had to go on the disabled list. Vinny responded with 24 hits in 60 at-bats for a .400 average and put together a 12-game hitting streak before spraining his ankle on May 19 in San Diego. Vinny came back in June and batted .262 in the month, with his biggest day in the majors to that point coming June 23. That night, he and catcher Danny Sheaffer drove in five runs

Growing up in Mexico, and throughout his minor-league career, Vinny played shortstop exclusively.

each; Vinny hit two home runs, scored four runs and had 10 total bases in a 15-5 win over the Cincinnati Reds.

Vinny went into a slump in July, when he batted only .167. He didn't get his first RBI away from Mile High Stadium until August 2, when he hit a two-run homer in Cincinnati. For the season, he hit .305 at Mile High Stadium but only .206 on the road, and finished at .255 with nine homers and 30 RBIs in 337 at-bats in 105 games.

The Rockies finished their first season in last place in the National League West with a 67-95 record. Like Vinny, the team went into a huge slump in July and early August, losing 13 in a row and 20 of 23 after the All-Star break. But from August 8 until the end of the season, they showed dramatic improvement, winning 31 of their final 52 games. The most noteworthy development of the Rockies' first season was the amazing fan support at Mile High Stadium, where they drew a major-league record 4,483,350 fans, or an average of 55,350 per game.

"I had played in front of 50,000 people before, but never 75–80,000," Vinny said. "It was very exciting. That was a great year for me. The fans were great, and it was my first full season in the big leagues."

Near the end of that season, another big event occurred. Vinny was introduced to his future wife, Samantha Owen, by her sister, who had sold Vinny a cellular phone. After the 1993 season, Vinny returned to Mexico for part of the winter and played

for Obregon of the Mexican Winter League. That is a practice he continues even today, primarily because he feels he owes it to the people of his native country to have the opportunity to see him play.

"I do that for the fans," Vinny said. "Especially in Obregon. They have known me since I was a

Vinny and Samantha were married on March 9, 1995. Their only child, Vinicio Jr. was born on March 12, 1996.

puppy. To see me now as an All-Star, they love that. They pack the stadium. I want to play for them. And I just love to play baseball. A lot of players like to golf or fish or hunt. Those things don't attract me much. By about November, I'm ready to play again. Baseball is my career, but it's my hobby, too."

Vinny went into the 1994 season as the backup shortstop once again, but this time he found himself behind a new starter, Walt Weiss. The Rockies had signed the veteran shortstop as a free agent to stabilize the defense up the middle and to bat leadoff. With Weiss playing every day, there was little opportunity for Vinny to get into the lineup. He appeared in only nine games in the first five weeks of the season, going 1 for 10. With Nelson Liriano, a more versatile veteran also on the roster as a backup infielder, and with pitcher Kent Bottenfield returning from the disabled list, the Rockies decided to send Vinny back to their Triple-A farm team in Colorado Springs.

"I was very disappointed," Vinny said. "They didn't give me a chance to do anything. I didn't have a position. They wanted to give Roberto Mejia a chance to play second base. I never thought I would have to go back to the minors again. But I didn't get discouraged. They told me I would be playing all the infield positions, and I went and worked at it as hard as I could."

After hitting .244 with one home run and 11 RBIs in 22 games at Colorado Springs, Vinny was called back to the Rockies on June 4, when the club decided to demote Mejia, who had fallen into a deep offensive slump. Vinny started hitting from the minute he came back, and Baylor kept finding places to put him in the lineup. Over the rest of the season, Vinny started 13 games at shortstop, 12 at second base, six at third base and two at first base after Andres Galarraga suffered a broken hand. Vinny hit .374 for the rest of the season, which came to an abrupt halt on August 11, when major-league players went on strike because of a dispute with team owners.

But Vinny's work wasn't finished. The Rockies asked him to go to their instructional league operation in Tucson, Arizona, after the season to work on playing third base. Under the tutelage of infield instructor Gene Glynn, Vinny spent 10 days there.

"I was eating breakfast one morning and Gebhard called me," Vinny said. "He said they wanted me to learn third base just in case Charlie Hayes didn't come back next year. I didn't think the strike would last as long as it did. I wanted to be ready. I worked hard."

Said Gebhard: "He didn't have to go, but he did. And he worked his butt off. We thought he would be able to play third base. His arm was fine. We weren't worried about that. The thing we were worried about was that first step after the ball was hit. That's the thing we worked on."

The strike lingered on into the following spring training. Meanwhile, Vinny married Samantha on March 9, 1995. Not only did Samantha help Vinny to further develop his English skills, she also picked up Spanish and speaks it fluently. The couple's first and only child, Vinicio Jr., was born March 12, 1996.

When the strike was settled in late April of 1995 and camps opened again for big-league players, a development occurred that changed Vinny's career path.

CHAPTER FIVE
Everyday Player

The scenario that Gebhard and the Rockies envisioned occurred. Charlie Hayes left the club as a free agent, leaving third base open. Since the Rockies had already spent $22 million to sign right fielder Larry Walker as a free agent and another $13 million to sign pitcher Bill Swift, it was decided that Vinny would get a chance to replace Hayes. And that was just fine with Vinny.

"It was the chance I was looking for," he said. "I thought I could play every day in the big leagues, but nobody had given me the opportunity."

Said Gebhard: "We decided it was time to turn the page. I said, 'Why don't we give Vinny a chance?' We were a little worried going into that spring training. But we thought, let's see what happens, and if it doesn't work out, we'll try somebody else. The rest is history."

To say Vinny adjusted quickly would be an understatement. After a slow start during which he hit only .179 without a home run through 10 games, Vinny got comfortable and started hitting. Three months later, he found himself starting in the All-Star Game, replacing San Francisco's Matt Williams, who had been voted in by the fans but was injured and couldn't play.

"It was tough for me early," Vinny said. "If I went 0 for 3, Don would pinch-hit for me. My confidence wasn't good. But I had a big game against Florida. I hit two homers and drove in six runs, and that boosted my confidence. I knew I could do it. I didn't look back anymore. I took off from there."

Vinny was named National League Player of the Week May 8-14, when he batted .609 (14 for 23) with four homers and 14 RBIs. He started June with a 13-game hitting streak in which he hit .451 (23 for 51) with six doubles, five home runs, 12 runs scored and 14 RBIs. For the month, he hit in 24 of 27 games and batted .324.

Just before the All-Star break, Vinny hit two homers on consecutive nights against Montreal, the first time that had been done in club history. That brought his first-half totals to .317 with 17 homers and 48 RBIs, and it was enough to convince Expos manager Felipe Alou, who was also the National League All-Star manager that year, to name Vinny as the starting third baseman.

"I felt great," Vinny said. "Nobody thought I could play every day the year before. But Bob Gebhard saw something in me, and thought I could do it. It was nice to get the opportunity to prove it.

I'll always appreciate the Rockies organization for giving me the chance. In spring training, I never thought anything about the All-Star Game. It's unbelievable."

The game was played in the new Ballpark at Arlington that season, and in sweltering 100-degree heat. Vinny went hitless in his two at-bats, striking out against Kevin Appier and grounding out to third against Dennis Martinez, but that didn't dampen his enthusiasm.

Vinny's move to third base came at the start of the 1995 season. He also started in the All-Star game at third base that year.

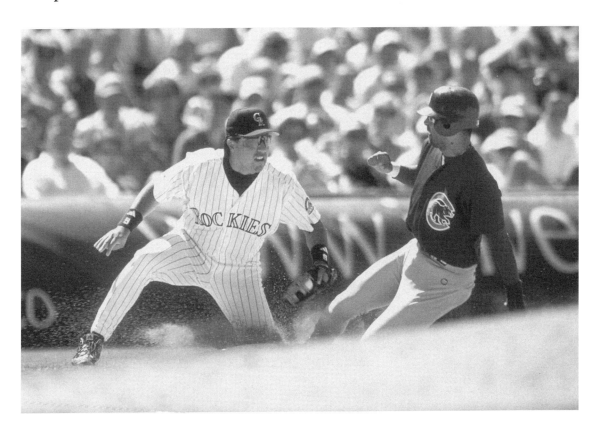

"I enjoyed every second of it," Vinny said. "My wife was pregnant at the time. Everything was going great for me."

Vinny's second half was much like the first, as he hit .302 with 15 homers and 42 RBIs after the break. He finished at .309 with 32 homers and 90 RBIs in a season that was shortened to 144 games. One of the biggest hits of the second half was a game-winning two-run homer off Chicago's Turk Wendell that gave the Rockies a 4-2 win on August 20.

Vinny was especially dangerous at the Rockies' new home park, Coors Field, where he batted .383. After the season, he was honored with the Silver Slugger Award, which goes to the best offensive player at each position. Vinny also was very good defensively, as he committed only 15 errors and had a .958 fielding percentage.

His final numbers were the best in a season by a Mexican native, breaking the marks of Aurelio Rodriguez, a third baseman who had spent 17 years in the majors in the 1960s and 1970s. Rodriguez hit .237 with 124 home runs and 648 RBIs in his career, and his best individual year was 1971 with Detroit, when he hit 19 homers and drove in 83 runs.

"That winter, we were playing in Los Moches when they retired his number," Vinny said of Rodriguez. "He said, 'You broke all my records. Now I want you to break my other record—17 years in the big leagues.'"

Vinny gave at least part of the credit for his successful season to Rockies hitting instructor Art Howe, now the manager of the Oakland A's. It was Howe who helped instill in Vinny the idea of not trying to pull every pitch, and instead try to hit pitches on the outside part of the plate to right field.

"No matter who gets the credit, Vinny did the work," Baylor said. "He made it happen with all the work he put in."

With their new park located on Blake and 20th Streets in downtown Denver, and with continued fan support that was unsurpassed in baseball history, the Rockies' summer turned into a memorable one. The team was filled with sluggers such as Ellis Burks, Andres Galarraga, Larry Walker, Dante Bichette and Vinny, and that group picked up the nickname the Blake Street Bombers.

Vinny, who batted sixth in the order, did his part by being one of the four Rockies regulars to bat .300, and one of four to hit at least 30 homers—only the second time that had occurred in major-league history. Vinny was the second of the foursome to reach 30, connecting on August 24. Bichette led the team with 40 homers as part of a season that earned him second place in the National League Most Valuable Player balloting. Walker (36) and Galarraga (31) also did it.

In fact, most National League offensive categories had Rockies at or near the top. Bichette finished first in home runs, hits, RBIs and slugging percentage. Vinny was fifth in home runs, seventh in batting average, eighth in hits, seventh in doubles and sixth in slugging percentage. Walker was second in home runs and slugging percentage, and Galarraga was third in RBIs and eighth in homers. It all added up to the most potent offense in baseball.

What made Vinny's accomplishment special was that the other three sluggers are all 6-foot-3 and weigh from 225 pounds, but Vinny is two inches shorter and weighs just 205 pounds.

"You look at his physique and you don't think he has that kind of power," Baylor said. "You don't see him in the weight room. A lot of guys do heavy lifting, but Vinny doesn't have to. One great thing for him was having Galarraga around. Vinny wasn't ready to step into the No. 4 spot in the order. The sixth spot was a comfortable one for him. Galarraga took the pressure off him. That helped him out a lot."

The Rockies got off to a surprisingly good start, winning seven of their first eight games, and remained in first place for all but 13 days of the first half of the season. They went into the All-Star break with a five-game winning streak that left them at 39-30, five games ahead in the National League West. They stayed in first place until August 13, when a loss at Atlanta dropped them to second, where they stayed for 14 of the next 16 days. A six-game winning streak put them back in first on September 11, and they stayed there until September 25.

Vinny celebrates a victory with his teammates. The Rockies' lone playoff appearance came in 1995.

The season boiled down to a final four-game series against the San Francisco Giants at Coors Field. The Giants won the first two games by scores of 12-4 and 10-7, dropping the Rockies two games behind with two games to play. But the Rockies also had a shot at the wild-card spot, since they were tied with the Houston Astros.

Things didn't look too promising on the final day of the season, when the Giants took an early 8-2 lead. But the Rockies rallied, and reliever Curtis Leskanic got the final three outs to preserve a 10-9 victory that set off a big celebration. The Rockies had reached the playoffs in only their third year of existence, five years faster than any other team.

"That was one of my best experiences in baseball," Vinny said. "To win that game against the Giants, and to see the fans and the faces of our players and Don Baylor. It was a great experience."

Ironically, the Rockies' opponent in the first round of the playoffs was Vinny's former team—the Atlanta Braves, who were the class of the National League that season. Heavily favored to advance to the World Series, the Braves eliminated the Rockies in four games, but the scrappy Rockies held the lead at some point in each game.

The Braves scored a run in the ninth inning to win the opener in Coors Field, 5-4. In that game,

Vinny hit a double and a two-run homer that gave the Rockies a 3-1 lead in the fourth inning. It was Vinny's two-run homer in Game 3 that broke a tie, and he also drove in the final run in the 10th inning of the Rockies' 7-5 victory. In the fourth and final game, Vinny hit another home run, but it wasn't enough in the 10-4 loss. In all, Vinny batted .467 with three homers and six RBIs in the series.

"I still have good feelings about the Braves," Vinny said. "When I play them, I try to beat them— just like I do anybody else. But they were the team that signed me out of Mexico, so I appreciate them for that."

After the season, the Rockies awarded Vinny with a two-year, $3 million contract. He soon would prove to be worth that and much more.

CHAPTER SIX
Mirror Images

Vinny prides himself on being a durable and consistently excellent player. But never before in major-league history had a player been as consistently excellent as Vinny was in the 1996 and 1997 seasons.

When his numbers were compared after both seasons, they were virtually identical. And in fact, in the three main offensive categories—batting average, home runs and RBIs—Vinny's numbers were exactly the same. In both seasons, he hit .304 with 40 homers and 113 RBIs.

"What people forget is I had 32 homers and 90 RBIs in 1995, and that season was shortened by 18 games," Vinny said. "I could have had another year of 40 homers and 100 RBIs. That shows I'm pretty consistent. That's what I want to be."

Vinny's 40th home run of the 1996 season didn't come until his final at-bat, when he connected off San Francisco's Mark Dewey in the sixth inning. Prior to that blast, Vinny had gone 12 games without one, and he clearly was pressing to hit No. 40.

The home run was historical in that it gave the Rockies three players with 40 or more homers, which had been done only one other time in major-league history, by Hank Aaron, Davey Johnson and Darrell Evans of the 1972 Atlanta Braves.

Galarraga led the National League with 47 homers, and Ellis Burks also hit 40 in a big year that ended with a third-place finish in the National League Most Valuable Player balloting. Vinny's 40th homer also was No. 221 for the Rockies that season, which tied a National League record for the most by a team in a single season.

Vinny waited until his final at-bat of the 1996 season to hit his 40th homer. He also hit 40 again in 1997.

"I was trying to hit one for so long," Vinny said. "That was all the media asked me about every day. I told myself I could do it. It came down to my last at-bat of the season, and I got a pitch to do it. I had two strikes on me, too."

Vinny, Galarraga, Burks and Bichette also each drove in least 100 runs, which tied a National League record. Unfortunately, the Rockies didn't take advantage of all their offensive fireworks, and they missed the playoffs.

They lost five of their first seven games and had a seven-game losing streak in May that dropped them into last place at 15-21. They did make it back into a tie for first on July 25, but four days later they were back in third place to stay.

The Rockies' 55-26 record at Coors Field was the second-best home record in baseball, but they struggled terribly on the road, going 28-53. That added up to a disappointing 83-79 finish, which was good enough only for third place in the National League West.

The other trend in Vinny's game that became evident in 1996 was his hitting first-pitch home runs. A total of 21 of his 40 homers came on the first pitch. Overall, Vinny batted .416 when he hit the first pitch. And from 1996 through 1998, 45 of Vinny's 126 homers were hit on the first pitch.

"I'm an aggressive hitter," Vinny said. "I swing at strikes. If it's a strike on the first pitch, I'm swinging. My first year, pitchers were trying to get ahead of me with fastballs on the first pitch, and I hit a lot of those. Now they throw me a lot of sliders and changeups on the first pitch. But if it's a strike, I'm swinging at it."

Vinny also hit the Rockies' only two grand slams of the season. The first came April 6 off Montreal's Kirk Rueter. His second climaxed the biggest comeback in club history, as the Rockies rallied after a long rain delay and erased a 9-2 deficit with an 11-run seventh inning against San Di-

Vinny gets caught in a rundown against the Montreal Expos.

ego on July 12. Vinny connected off former team-mate Willie Blair to give the Rockies the lead, and they eventually won 13-12.

Vinny had only five home runs through May, but got hot in June, when he belted 12 to bring his pre–All-Star break total to 17. From June 11 through June 30, Vinny homered in three consecutive games on three different occasions. The hot streak earned him National League Player of the Week honors June 10–16, when he batted .346 with four homers, eight RBIs and seven runs scored.

June also saw Vinny put together a 10-game hitting streak in which he batted .435 with six homers and 13 RBIs. In another 10-game hitting streak July 20–29, Vinny batted .405 with four homers and 11 RBIs. He was batting .305 with 56 RBIs at the break, but that wasn't enough to get him on the National League All-Star team. That honor went to Ken Caminiti of Houston, who went on to win the Most Valuable Player award, and Chipper Jones of Atlanta.

One game that meant almost as much to Vinny as the All-Star Game came July 15. That was when the Rockies played the Padres, and the starting pitchers were Mexican natives—Armando Reynoso and Fernando Valenzuela.

Prior to Vinny's rise to stardom, the most prominent players to come out of Mexico were predominantly pitchers. The best of them was Valenzuela, who had won the National League Rookie of the Year Award and the National League Cy Young Award in 1981 while pitching for the Los Angeles Dodgers; he went on to win 173 games.

"When I was a kid, Fernando was the idol to everyone in Mexico," Vinny said. "Every time he pitched, the game was on television in Mexico."

But when Vinny faced his former idol, he hit the first pitch over the right-center field wall at Coors Field for a home run. Reynoso out-pitched Valenzuela, and the Rockies won 8-4.

"It was great to see two Mexican pitchers in the same game," Vinny said. "Fernando was one of the greatest left-handed pitchers. To be able to face him and be a part of that game was great."

Vinny finished 1996 with new career highs in games played (160, missing only two), at-bats (629), runs scored (97), home runs (40), RBIs (113), walks (35) and stolen bases (7). He also slightly improved his fielding percentage to .960. He had similar numbers for the 1997 season, with 159 games played, 612 at-bats, 94 runs scored, 40 home runs, 113 RBIs, 44 walks, and 2 stolen bases.

The games played category was also impressive to Baylor: in a two-year period, Vinny had played in all but five games, and in three years as a regular, he had missed only 14 games.

Vinny displays the consistent swing that helped him produce three consecutive seasons of hitting at least .300, 40 homers, and 100 RBIs.

"Vinny and Galarraga, they never wanted to take a day off," Baylor said. "They were going to play every day. They looked at me like I had just kidnapped their kids or something if I didn't have them in the lineup. They're here to play every day."

Although his final numbers were virtually identical to those of 1996, Vinny got there in a different manner in 1997. He started off with one of the hottest months of his career, batting .360 with nine homers and 25 RBIs in April. He was named National League Player of the Week April 7–13, when he was 7 for 16 with two homers and seven RBIs.

But from that point until mid-July, Vinny went into a slump that dropped his batting average down to .282 at the All-Star break. Even though he had 22 homers and 64 RBIs at that point, the numbers weren't good enough for him to make the National League All-Star team for the second consecutive season.

That disappointment set him off on a hot streak after the break, as he hit .500 during a nine-game hitting streak July 17–26 that included a four-hit game and a five-hit game when he slugged two homers, drove in four runs and scored four runs against the Chicago Cubs at Wrigley Field.

Vinny also put together a career-best 22-game hitting streak from August 9 to September 1. In those 22 games, he batted .385 with eight homers and 16 RBIs and increased his batting average from .294 to .308. And this time, Vinny didn't wait until his last at-bat of the season to hit his 40th homer. That came September 16 in Miami off the Marlins' Kirk Ojala.

But like 1996, the Rockies were a disappointment in 1997. They jumped out in front in the National League West by going 17-7 in April and were 21-9 before they lost 11 of 13 games to fall back into third place. They moved up into second place on May 21 and stayed there until just before the All-Star break. But beginning July 1, they lost 15 of 16 games to fall to 44-54 and 10 1/2 games behind, and never were a factor again. They finished with an 83-79 record, just as they did in 1996.

Vinny is one of the most popular members of the Colorado Rockies with the fans at their home park, Coors Field.

The 1997 season also was disappointing for Vinny in that with the exception of 1990, it marked the first time since their days back in the Mexican League that he wasn't a team-mate of Reynoso. After the 1996 season, Reynoso became a free agent and signed with the New York Mets when the Rockies showed little interest in keeping him. The two best friends faced each other early in the 1997 season.

"That was very strange," Vinny said. "He's my best friend in baseball. We played our whole careers together until then. We played together in Saltillo, in the minors with the Braves, in the big leagues with the Braves, and with the Rockies. Winter ball, too."

Said Baylor: "You can't have any better professional guys from other countries than Vinny, Armando and Galarraga. If Vinny was here by himself, I don't know, would it have been different? I do know they helped him."

But by this time, Vinny was a star in his own right, and he was about to grow even brighter. In the off-season, he signed a new contract that would pay him $24 million over four years. He would live up to it in 1998 with a season for the ages.

CHAPTER SEVEN
Exclusive Company

L ike the Fourth of July, which celebrates the independence of the United States, Cinco de Mayo (the Fifth of May) celebrates Mexico's independence. Naturally, the day is an important one for Vinny. But in 1998, the day took on a significance of a different sort. Because at that point, Vinny found himself leading the major league in home runs with 14.

In the year of the home run, when both Mark McGwire and Sammy Sosa would break Roger Maris's long-standing record by slugging 70 and 66 respectively, and when Ken Griffey Jr. and Greg Vaughn would hit at least 50 homers, it was Vinny who was on top after the season's first five weeks. And with that position came newfound fame.

There was a feature on the television show *This Week In Baseball*, a big story in *Sports Illustrated*, and a full-page picture in a Denver newspaper of Vinny dressed up in the outfit of a matador. Even cab drivers in National League cities now knew who Vinny was and the numbers he was putting up.

"I kept telling everybody, the record isn't broken in April," Vinny said. "I got off to a great start with three homers in the first series in Arizona. A lot of it had to do with moving from sixth to fifth in the order. I had Todd Helton hitting behind me."

Baylor joked about all the coverage Vinny was receiving, saying, "Everybody thinks this is new. The guy has hit 40 homers the last two years."

One of those 14 early-season homers was a memorable game-winning blast off Houston's Billy Wagner on April 28, a solo shot in the ninth inning that gave the Rockies a 7-6 victory. That continued a trend of Vinny's hitting big home runs off the game's best relief pitchers in game-deciding situations.

It started in 1996, when Vinny turned around a 97-mph fastball from Philadelphia's Ricky Bottalico for a home run that gave the Rockies a 7-6 victory on June 21. On August 10 of that year, Vinny hit a two-run homer off Atlanta's Mark Wohlers, who often reached 100 mph with his fastball, to give the Rockies a 9-7 victory.

Later in the 1998 season, Wagner again challenged Vinny with a fastball, and Vinny responded with a three-run home run that was the difference in a 6-3 Rockies win on August 23. Two more game-winning homers came off Arizona's Gregg Olson on June 3 and Montreal's Ugueth Urbina on August 21. Vinny's ability to hit the hardest-throwing pitchers in the game prompted Rockies hitting instructor Clint Hurdle to say, "I think he could pull a bullet."

While Vinny didn't stay among sluggers such as McGwire and Sosa when it came to home runs, he did put together a season that deserved much attention. In fact, it was one of the greatest offensive seasons ever put together by a third baseman, and combined with his 1995–97 statistics, put Vinny in some very elite company for a four-year span: Only three other third basemen in major-league history hit more home runs in a season than Vinny's 1998 total of 46—Minnesota's Harmon Killebrew (49 in 1969), Philadelphia's Mike Schmidt (48 in 1980) and Milwaukee's Eddie Mathews (47 in 1953). Only one other third baseman in major-league history drove in more runs in a season than Vinny's 1998 total of 144—Cleveland's Al Rosen (145 in 1953). Vinny became one of only six players in major-league history to bat at least .300 and hit 40 or more homers in three consecutive years. The others were Babe Ruth (1926–32), Jimmie Foxx (1932–34), Ted Kluszewski (1953–55), Duke Snider (1953–55) and Galarraga, who did it the same three years as Vinny, 1996–98. Vinny also became one of only seven National League players to hit 40 homers in three consecutive seasons, joining Ralph Kiner (1947–51), Duke Snider (1953–57), Eddie Mathews (1953–55), Kluszewski (1953–55), Ernie Banks (1957–60) and Galarraga (1996–98). And Vinny joined a group of only 15 players in history to hit .300 or better with at least 30 homers in four consecutive years.

Along the way in 1998, Vinny played in all 162 games to extend his consecutive games played streak to 247, passed Jorge Orta to become Mexico's all-time major-league home run leader with 170,

Vinny's 1998 season was one of the best ever by a third baseman, and cemented his place as one of the game's top players. Here, he greets some of his many fans.

and participated in the Home Run Derby and All-Star Game held at Coors Field. In all, it was a magical year that validated Vinny as one of the game's great players.

"I'm proud of the player I've become," Vinny said. "Nobody ever thought I could become the kind of player I am. When my big-league career started, nobody was saying that I would be an All-Star. Five years ago, I was just trying to stay in the big leagues. I had to earn everything. Nothing was given to me. I had to do it. I feel so proud."

Vinny earned a spot in the All-Star Game with a big first half in which he hit .307 with 25 home runs and 75 RBIs. He calls the All-Star experience in front of the Denver fans one of the top highlights of his major-league career.

"It was beautiful," Vinny said. "The ovation they gave me in the home-run contest, and then the next night in the game, it gave me chills. Your eyes water a little bit. It was a great experience." In the home-run hitting contest, Vinny was one of four players to hit seven homers in the first round, one fewer than leader Ken Griffey Jr. of Seattle. In the second round, Vinny slammed five more, but Griffey and Jim Thome of Cleveland hit eight to advance to the finals. Griffey won the contest. In the All-Star Game, Vinny started along with team-mate Larry Walker, and went hitless in two at-bats with a pop out and a flyout, leaving him 0 for 4 in All-Star Game competition. Vinny started another hitting streak immediately after the All-Star break, driving in a run in 10 of his first 11 games and hitting in 14 consecutive games July 13-27. For the month of July, Vinny batted .381 with 12 homers and 25 RBIs, tying a club record for home runs in a month.

More milestones were reached in the season's final two months. Vinny topped the 100-RBI mark

Vinny, Samantha, and Vinny Jr. sit in front of the sign at Vinny Castilla Field, which was built in the Denver area with the help of a large donation from Vinny.

for the third consecutive season on August 4 and went on to finish with 144. Exactly one month later, he had a two-homer game against San Diego, giving him a career high on his way to 46. Vinny's final homer was a two-run blast off San Francisco's Julian Tavarez that gave the Rockies a late-inning lead and capped a seven-run comeback. Vinny's 200th hit came September 10 against San Diego, and it was a home run. He would finish with a career-high 206 hits. It all added up to his second Silver Slugger Award.

The Rockies, however, again were a disappointment despite Vinny's great season and Larry Walker's winning the National League batting title. They struggled to a 3-10 home stand in April to drop to 7-13 and eight games out of first place on April 20; they remained stuck no higher than fourth place the rest of the season. In their worst season since they were inaugurated in 1993, the Rockies finished 77-85; as a result, Baylor was fired the day after the season ended. Baylor would land a job for 1999 as the hitting instructor for the Atlanta Braves, from where he still looks fondly upon Vinny.

"I'm glad it's all worked out for him," Baylor said. "Certain guys, you hope it works out for. Vinny deserves what he's gotten. He's come from a backup guy to a star player. Now he's a perennial All-Star.

He's an amazing story. But he still loves to play, no matter how much money he makes. He's a special guy."

Vinny has lots of reasons to smile. His last several seasons have been wonderful and his baseball career affords him and his family a very comfortable life.

After his smashing return to Mexico to open the 1999 season, Vinny went through some tough times both on and off the field. The spring began with the news of Galarraga, one of Vinny's closest friends, being stricken with cancer. Vinny's wife, Samantha, suffered two miscarriages in the first half of the season, and his mother fell and broke her arm back home in Oaxaca. Vinny also was bothered by a back injury that brought his consecutive games streak to an end, and also adversely affected his swing and his fielding ability.

Although the numbers would be quite good for most other players, Vinny was considered to be having an off year through the All-Star break, which he entered with a .280 batting average, 19 homers, 57 RBIs and 14 errors—one more than in all of 1998. "It's been a tough year, mentally," Vinny said in late July. "I know you have to perform. You're a professional. But when stuff is going on with your friends and your family, it's tough not to think about it. It takes your mind off playing. The back injury affects me, too. The best thing I have is my bat speed. When that slows down, you get into bad habits."

Vinny finished the season with 33 home runs and 102 RBIs—one of four Rockies hitters to reach the 30-homer and 100-RBI marks. That gave him five consecutive years with more than 30 homers.

But his batting average dipped to .275, the first time in six seasons that he didn't hit at least .300, and his error total was a team-high 19.

Vinny's struggles, along with yet another disappointing season by the Rockies, brought about speculation that several players were involved in trades leading up to the July 31 deadline. But the deadline passed and Vinny remained with the Rockies, although the San Diego Padres were one team that expressed interest in acquiring him. Vinny knows that few players stay in one place over their careers, but he would have been very happy if he had remained with the Rockies until he retired—as it turned out, that was not to be the case.

After the 1999 season ended and the team hired a new general manager, several major changes were made. Vinny was traded to the Tampa Bay Devil Rays in a nine-player, four-team deal. "I loved this organization," Vinny said of the Colorado Rockies. "They gave me a chance to establish myself in the big leagues. But I want to be where I'm wanted, like Tampa Bay."

MAJOR LEAGUE STATS

Year	Team	G	AB	R	H	2B	3B	HR	RBI	SB	AV
1991	At	12	5	1	1	0	0	0	0	0	.20(
1992	At	9	16	1	4	1	0	0	1	0	.25(
1993	Col	105	337	36	86	9	7	9	30	2	.25!
1994	Col	52	130	16	43	11	1	3	18	2	.33:
1995	Col	139	527	82	163	34	2	32	90	2	.30!
1996	Col	160	629	97	191	34	0	40	113	7	.304
1997	Col	159	612	94	186	25	2	40	113	2	.304
1998	Col	162	645	108	206	28	4	46	144	5	.31!
1999	Col	158	615	83	169	24	1	33	102	2	.27!
Totals		956	3516	518	1049	166	17	203	611	22	.28(

CHRONOLOGY

1967 Born in Oaxaca, Mexico, July 4th

1985 Graduated from Carlos Gracida Institute, was the baseball team's most valuable player; attended Benito Juárez University

1987 Signs first pro contract with Saltillo Sarapemakers of the Mexican League

1989 Atlanta Braves purchase his contract from Saltillo

1991 Gets first major-league hit, a single off Xavier Hernandez

1992 Selected by the Colorado Rockies in the expansion draft

1995 Marries Samantha Owen, March 9; hits .309 with 32 homers and 90 RBIs and makes the All-Star Game in his first season as an everyday player; follows that up by hitting .467 with three homers in a division series against Atlanta

1996 Vinicio Jr. born March 12; becomes one of only three Rockies to hit 40 homers in a season, only the second trio of teammates to do so in major-league history

1997 In an amazing coincidence that shows his consistency, he hits .304 with 40 homers and 113 RBIs for the second consecutive season

1998 Drives in 144 runs, most by a third baseman in National League history, and second to Cleveland's Al Rosen in major-league history

1999 Hit 33 homers, giving him five consecutive years of 30 or more home runs

INDEX